vegetarian

First published in 2012 by

New Holland Publishers

London • Sydney • Cape Town • Auckland

www.newhollandpublishers.com

Garfield House 86–88 Edgware Road London W2 2EA United Kingdom

1/66 Gibbes Street Chatswood NSW 2067 Australia

Wembley Square First Floor Solan Road Gardens Cape Town 8001 South Africa

218 Lake Road Northcote Auckland New Zealand

A catalogue record of this book is available at the British Library and the National Library of Australia

ISBN: 9781742573502

Publisher: Fiona Schultz

Publishing director: Lliane Clarke

Design: Tracy Loughlin

Production director: Olga Dementiev

Printer: Toppan Leefung Printing Limited

10 9 8 7 6 5 4 3 2 1

Follow New Holland Publishers on

Facebook: www.facebook.com/NewHollandPublishers

contents

Introduction

This book celebrates the joy of seasonal foods and the freedom of meat-free meals. Being a vegetarian doesn't mean giving anything up. It's about embracing the natural bounty of the fruits, seeds and leaves of the plants that humanity has always enjoyed. Vegetarian offers nearly 90 exciting recipes, from quick snacks to family meals and dishes for entertaining.

Cereals

Rice is the world's largest crop and is grown on every inhabited continent. Long-grain rice, such as basmati rice from India and Pakistan, is great steamed and makes a fragrant bed for vegetable casseroles and curries. From Italy comes Arborio rice, which absorbs the beautiful flavours of the stock in which it's cooked to make risotto.

Brown rice has not had its husk removed and takes longer to cook. Many people, however, enjoy its nutty taste and make it part of a fibre-rich diet. Rice can be cooked ahead of time and reheated, and leftovers can be transformed into tempting treats such as rice balls or fried rice. Store cooked rice by covering it with plastic wrap after it has cooled, and placing it in the refrigerator for up to three days.

From corn we get traditional dishes like polenta and grits. Corn on the cob can be steamed or boiled, and the kernels cut away with a sharp knife and added to salads for a bright and nutritious touch. Some like to get back to basics and cook corn in its own husk over the glowing embers of a fire. However you enjoy corn, it's a good source of vitamin C and fibre

Whole grains like barley take some time to cook, but make a hearty part of a winter soup and a toothsome addition to a salad. Barley is an excellent source of fibre and niacin. It's also worth considering trying other grains, such as wild rice. Grown in North America, wild rice is more costly than ordinary rice, but can be used sparingly to add nutty highlights to soups and salads. Buckwheat, although not a true cereal, has a wonderful earthy flavour and its flour can be used in pancakes or mixed with wheat flour to make pasta.

Whole grains keep very well in a tightly sealed container for up to a year if stored in a cool, dry, dark place. They should be rinsed before using and picked over for small stones or sticks. If you're removing them from the packet, you can cut out part of the label and stick it on the lid so you always know what's inside.

Processed grains such as flour and oatmeal don't last as long and should be used within 6 months. These, too, need to be stored in tightly sealed containers.

Fresh from the Dairy

Fresh milk and mature cheeses, churned butter and cultured yoghurt are some of our favourite foods. Many people have fond childhood memories of a white milk 'moustache' being left on their faces after gulping down glasses of cold milk to strengthen their growing bones.

Some dairy products, such as butter or French Brie cheese, can contain high levels of fat and

salt. In moderation, however, these treats can be a delicious part of a well-balanced diet. People on restricted diets should consult their health professional about consuming dairy products.

Throughout our lives, we need calcium, and dairy products provide a good source of readily absorbed calcium. Some nutritionists recommend consuming the equivalent of two glasses of milk a day. Milk is not only a good source of calcium, but also of phosphorus and protein. Fresh milk is always best purchased regularly and stored in the refrigerator away from strong-smelling foods.

Cream can be used to enrich sauces or smother sweet dishes such as ripe summer strawberries or fresh bakery goods. It's high in fat though—between 18 per cent and 35 per cent—so it's best enjoyed in moderation.

Yoghurt is a cultured dairy product that has all the pros of whole milk with the possibility of added benefits from micro-flora such as lactobacillus, sometimes referred to as 'helpful bugs'. They aid digestion and keep the gut healthy. To find yoghurt with these healthy bugs, look for the term 'live cultures' on the label.

Yoghurt can be mixed with mashed avocado and a sprinkle of sea salt to make guacamole, dolloped over a baked potato and topped with chopped chives, or just spooned over fresh fruit and drizzled with honey for a great breakfast.

The cheese family is a large one, ranging from all-time favourites such as Cheddar to soft Bocconcini, and luscious triple-cream Bries. Then, of course, there are the wonderful hard and nutty Parmesans from Italy, which are perfect for grating over pastas or finely shaving over fresh, leafy green salads.

Fresh cheeses are the lightest of the cheese family, as they contain more moisture and therefore have a lower fat ratio. As they're fresh and not matured, they're usually made with less salt. Ricotta is made from whey (liquid left over from making other cheese), has 30 per cent of the fat of hard cheese and is a good source of calcium. It can be spread straight onto biscuits or mixed with chopped herbs to make a quick dip. Or try flavouring it with a little grated Parmesan cheese, stuffing it into pasta shells and smothering them in tomato sauce. Sweetened with a little sugar and lemon rind, ricotta also makes a wonderful pancake filling.

A good supply of Cheddar, Edam, Colby, Monterey Jack or other popular cheese is great to have on hand. These cheeses are perfect to snack on, excellent thinly sliced as a sandwich filling, and brilliant grated into a salad or melted over corn chips or a breadcrumb topping.

More adventurous cheese-lovers can enjoy a cheese platter at the end of the meal—just like the French, who serve an array of cheeses such Camembert or blue cheese with a few biscuits between main course and dessert. Diners cut off a small wedge of each cheese and enjoy the rich tastes and aromas.

Pulses

If there was ever an award for the perfect whole vegetarian food, pulses would proudly claim the title.

Pulses, also known as legumes, are the dried seeds of plants from a family that includes beans, peas and lentils. They're an extremely nutritious food, containing 20 per cent fibre and 6–8 per cent protein. The really good news is that, apart from soybeans, pulses contain next to no fat and no cholesterol. They're also extremely versatile: the recipes in this book range from light dips to hearty loaves that are perfect for feeding a hungry crowd.

Some pulses, such as chickpeas, require soaking overnight in cold water. Others, like lentils and split peas, can be cooked in stock or water relatively quickly. Canned cooked pulses are a convenient way of keeping nutritious food at your fingertips.

All pulses are best stored in a sealed container in a dry, cool and dark place: that way they'll keep for up to 12 months.

Chickpeas react to rapid changes in heat by toughening up. If you're adding cooked chickpeas to a boiling pot, add a cup of cold water just before doing so.

Soybeans are one of the best-known pulses in the world. Although they're generally not called for in Western cooking, products made from the humble soybean are used every day. They're used to make hundreds of different foods and drinks, from soymilk to tofu to fermented products such as soy sauce and miso.

Tofu is a curd made from soybeans, and is slightly nutty, but it's best known for taking on the flavours of the sauces with which it's cooked. It's a great source of magnesium, calcium, phosphorus and iron.

When preparing dried pulses, pick over them and remove any discoloured ones and small stones. Rinse them under cold water and soak them according to the directions on the packet. Some people recommend soaking them in the fridge to stop them from fermenting – eating pulses that have fermented can cause upset tummies! The skins of pulses can toughen up when cooked with salt or acid, too, so it's a good idea to add salt or acidic ingredients like tomatoes halfway through the cooking time

Beans

Beans are one of nature's most versatile foods. They can be used to make a quick dip, enrich a soup, be cooked with spices to make a sauce for tacos or cooked with other vegetables to enhance the absorption of their rich nutrients and add warm earthy flavours.

Haricot beans (navy beans) are handy for stews and soups but are most famous for their starring role in baked beans. Many people love the deep burgundy colour of borlotti beans (roman beans), which are perfect for a vegetable minestrone. When cooked and cooled, dressed with salt, lemon juice, olive oil, chopped parsley and onions rings, they make a great salad. One of the best ways to enjoy broad beans (fava beans) is to make a delicious and healthy purée, a dish that is enjoyed around the Mediterranean as an accompaniment to vegetable kebabs or as a dip with crudités.

Across Europe, the Middle East and Asia, lentils are a traditional food. Served with rice, they provide a balanced meal, rich in protein, carbohydrate and essential minerals and vitamins. Being so small, lentils are fast to cook and can make wonderful dishes – from fragrant curries to hearty burgers and loaves.

Vegetables, Fruit and Nuts

Fruit and vegetables are at their nutritious best when picked at their ripest and eaten fresh. There's a sense of excitement in the markets every summer as the first of the local berries come in from the farms.

Every autumn, when the new season's apples are delivered from the orchards, people clamour to see who can get the first box. In winter, just after the early frosts, the carrots become sweeter and tastier; in spring there's a flourish of asparagus, the first new potatoes and spring greens. Eating with the seasons is not only the tastiest way of enjoying fruit and vegetables, it's also the most economical, as when there's a bountiful supply of fruit and vegetables, the prices go down.

Modern transport, however, allows us to enjoy fresh fruit and vegetables all year round. If you have time, regular trips to the market or greengrocer several times a week will mean you always have your produce at its freshest. Store green, leafy vegetables in plastic or paper bags to stop them losing moisture and goodness. Don't store fruit and vegetables together, as gases from the fruit will make some vegetables, such as broccoli and cabbage, turn yellow. Mushrooms should be stored flat in a single layer, stalk side up, in a paper bag.

Carbohydrate-rich vegetables such as potatoes are an economical way of filling up a crowd, but should be served with other vegetables or in a salad for a more balanced meal.

The good news is that leafy green vegetables have really good amounts of folate, and yellow and orange vegetables such as carrots and pumpkin have high levels of health-giving betacarotene.

Without a doubt, fresh fruit makes the healthiest choice of all snacks. A large bowl of fresh fruit on the kitchen bench or table allows family members to have a nutritious treat any time of the day they like. It's a good practice to get children eating fruit on a daily basis, instead of letting them reach for chocolate and other sugary treats. Fruit can be stored for a week or so in the crisper of the refrigerator if carefully wrapped, but it's more appetising if you allow it to return to room temperature before eating.

The natural fructose in ripe fresh fruit can be a great counterbalance of flavour. Crisp pears and apples are perfect to serve with cheese, and pears are a great addition to leafy green salads with a shaving of Parmesan cheese.

Tree nuts such as almonds, walnuts and hazelnuts are high in unsaturated oils and excellent sources of dietary fibre, vitamins and minerals. Tree nuts are ready for harvest at the end of autumn. Their hard outer shells can be difficult to crack open, so thankfully they're available at the market in plastic packs!

Peanuts actually grow underground, and as they belong to the pea family, they're a good source of protein. Because of the large proportion of oil in nuts they can easily go rancid, so buy small amounts of nuts frequently and store them in airtight containers.

The crunchy texture and nutty taste of seeds such as sesame seeds and sunflower seeds add a delicious touch to salads and vegetable dishes, and mean they're great as a topping for baked goods.

Use nuts and seeds straight from the pack or add an extra hit of flavour by toasting them: spread them evenly on a flat ovenproof tray and cook in a moderate oven for 2–10 minutes, depending on the size and quantity of the seeds or nuts. Allow them to become golden but not brown: don't leave them unattended, as they can burn quite quickly.

A Touch of Spice

Many of the world's great cuisines use spices and herbs to flavour their vegetables dishes.

Spicy does not necessarily mean hot! The sensation of heat comes from cooking with some of the more robust spices such as pepper and chilli.

Chilli, in moderation, adds a lively kick for a bit of variety. A small cinnamon stick or a few cloves or cardamom pods tossed into a slow-cooked bean dish can add a wonderful fragrant, exotic touch. And the old favourites of parsley, sage, rosemary and thyme are always great to cook with. A handful of coarsely chopped parsley will lighten and enliven any savoury dish. Sage, perhaps fried in a little butter, is the natural companion of potatoes. A pot of beans

cooked low and slow will enjoy the company of a small sprig of rosemary, and thyme goes well with baked tomatoes and slow-cooked dishes. In summer, fresh basil, tomatoes and a little olive oil make a classic salad.

Dried herbs are more concentrated than fresh herbs, so you'll need less of them. Keep spices and dried herbs well sealed in a dry, cool, dark place. Fresh herbs should be wrapped and kept for a few days in the crisper in the fridge. There's also a real joy in having a few pots or a patch of garden close to the kitchen dedicated to growing herbs. When you need a splash of green herbs, you simply pick what you need – fresh, vibrant and flavoursome.

Enjoy the bounty of the seasons in the right quantities:
• Buy small amounts of fresh dairy, fruit, vegetables and nuts frequently, and store them well
• Buy fruit and vegetables when they're at their freshest and ripest, and ask your greengrocer how to store them best
• Remember to mix up the recipes that you cook day-to-day for nutritional variety and different flavours

starters

Crudités with Herb Dip

serves 10

a selection of vegetables, such as broccoli and cauliflower florets, carrot sticks and baby new potatoes

HERB DIP

1 tablespoon fresh parsley, chopped

1 tablespoon fresh basil, chopped

¼ cup mayonnaise

⅓ cup sour cream

1 teaspoon Dijon mustard

freshly ground black pepper

Steam the vegetables separately until just tender. Drain, refresh under cold running water, drain again and set aside.

To make the dip, place parsley, basil, mayonnaise, sour cream, mustard and black pepper to taste in a food processor or blender and process to combine.

Arrange the vegetables on a large platter and accompany with dip.

Note This dip is delicious served with any lightly cooked or steamed vegetables. You might like to try serving snowpeas, zucchini, asparagus or cucumber instead.

Spiced Olives

serves 6

500g (1lb) green or ripe olives

1 sprig fresh oregano

1 sprig fresh thyme

1 teaspoon fresh rosemary, finely chopped

2 bay leaves

1 teaspoon fennel seeds, bruised

1 teaspoon cumin seeds, finely crushed

1 fresh red chilli, deseeded and chopped

4 cloves garlic, crushed

Using a small sharp knife, make a lengthwise slit through to pit of each olive. Put olives into a bowl. Stir in oregano, thyme, rosemary, bay leaves, fennel seeds, cumin seeds, chilli and garlic.

Into a jar with a tight-fitting lid, pack olive mixture. Add enough oil to cover olives, seal and leave at least 3 days, shaking jar occasionally

Roasted Red Pepper Raita

serves 4

2 red capsicums (bell peppers)

2 teaspoons cumin seeds

200g (7oz) Greek yoghurt

2 tablespoons fresh mint, finely chopped

salt and black pepper

1 teaspoon paprika to garnish

Preheat the grill to high. Cut the capsicums, lengthwise into quarters, then remove the seeds and grill, skin-side up, for 10 minutes or until blackened and blistered. Place in a plastic bag and leave to cool for 10 minutes.

Meanwhile, preheat a wok and dry-fry the cumin seeds, stirring constantly, over a high heat for 30 seconds, or until they start to pop. Remove the skins from the grilled capsicum and discard, then roughly chop the flesh.

Mix the capsicum with the yoghurt, cumin seeds and mint and season to taste. Transfer to a serving dish and garnish with the paprika.

Arancini Balls

makes 16

1 tablespoon olive oil

1 onion, finely chopped

1½ cups Arborio rice

½ teaspoon ground turmeric

3 cups vegetable stock

½ teaspoon chilli powder

freshly ground black pepper

3 spring onions, finely chopped

15g (½oz) butter

3 tablespoons Cheddar cheese, grated

2 eggs, lightly beaten

125g (4oz) Mozzarella cheese, cut into 16 cubes

¾ cup dried breadcrumbs

oil for deep-frying

Heat olive oil in a frying pan, add onion and cook for 3 minutes until soft. Stir in rice and turmeric and cook, stirring, for 2 minutes until rice is coated with oil.

Pour ¾ cup stock into the frying pan and bring to the boil. Cook, stirring frequently, until liquid has almost evaporated. Add chilli powder, black pepper to taste and remaining stock and simmer for 10–15 minutes or until liquid has been absorbed and rice is tender. Remove pan from heat and stir in spring onions, butter and Cheddar cheese.

Fold eggs into rice mixture, taking care not to mash the grains. Divide the mixture into 16 equal portions, then take a cheese cube and, using wet hands, mould one portion of rice around a cheese cube to form a ball. Repeat with remaining rice and cheese.

Roll balls in breadcrumbs, place on a plate lined with plastic wrap and refrigerate for 30 minutes. Heat oil in a deep saucepan until a cube of bread dropped in browns in 50 seconds, and cook 4–5 rice balls at a time for 5 minutes or until golden. Using a slotted spoon, remove balls and drain on absorbent kitchen paper. Serve immediately.

Tzatziki

makes 1 cup

185g (6½oz) plain Greek yoghurt

90g (3oz) cucumber, grated

1 tablespoon lemon juice

1 clove garlic, crushed

salt and black pepper

1 tablespoon mint, chopped

Combine all the ingredients in a bowl. Cover the bowl with cling wrap and refrigerate for at least 1 hour to allow the flavours to develop.

Serve with pita bread as a dip, or as an accompaniment sauce.

Spinach and Goat's Cheese Pita Pizza

serves 4

125g (4oz) sun-dried tomatoes in oil, drained, plus 2 tablespoons oil from the jar

2 tablespoons tomato paste

1 clove garlic, roughly chopped

2 teaspoons fresh thyme, finely chopped

250g (9oz) baby spinach

6 mini pita breads

6 cherry tomatoes, quartered

100g (3½oz) soft goat's cheese, sliced

1 tablespoon sesame seeds

Preheat the oven to 230°C (450°F). Blend the sun-dried tomatoes, tomato paste and garlic to a purée in a food processor or by using a hand blender. Mix in the thyme.

Bring a pan of water to the boil, immerse the spinach then remove and refresh in a bowl of cold water. Drain, then drizzle the sun-dried tomato oil over the top.

Spread the tomato and garlic purée over the pita breads and top with the spinach. Scatter the cherry tomatoes over, along with the cheese and sesame seeds. Cook for 10 minutes or until the cheese has melted slightly and started to brown.

Red Bean Dip

serves 4

2 tablespoons vegetable oil

1 small onion, chopped

1 clove garlic, crushed

1 fresh green chilli, deseeded and finely chopped

½ teaspoon chilli powder

440g (15oz) canned red kidney beans, drained, liquid reserved

50g (1¾oz) Cheddar cheese, grated

corn chips

Heat oil in a large frying pan, add onion, garlic, chilli and chilli powder and cook over a medium heat, stirring, for 3 minutes or until onion is soft.

Place all but 3 tablespoons of beans in a food processor or blender and process until smooth. Add bean purée and 2 tablespoons reserved liquid to pan, and mix well.

Stir in cheese and reserved beans and cook, stirring constantly, for 2–3 minutes or until cheese melts. Serve dip warm with corn chips.

Note This recipe can also be made using dried red kidney beans, but they'll need to be soaked and cooked first. After soaking, the water should be discarded and fresh water added for cooking. The beans must be boiled for 10 minutes first to remove haemagglutinins or toxins in the beans, which cause nausea, vomiting and diarrhoea. Then reduce the heat to a simmer and cook for 1¼–1½ hours or until tender.

Creamy Chickpea and Tomato Dip

serves 6

250g (9oz) dried chickpeas
(garbanzo beans)

6 tablespoons olive oil

finely grated zest of ½ lemon

juice of 2 lemons

350g (12oz) Roma tomatoes

2 cloves garlic, crushed

2 spring onions, finely chopped

3 tablespoons fresh parsley or
mint, finely chopped

salt and black pepper

Soak the chickpeas in cold water for 12 hours, or overnight. Drain and rinse thoroughly, then place in a saucepan and cover with fresh water. Bring to the boil and cook for 10 minutes, removing any foam with a slotted spoon. Reduce the heat and simmer, covered, for 1 hour or until tender.

Drain the chickpeas, reserving 6 tablespoons of the cooking water, and set a few chickpeas aside to garnish. In the food processor, blend the remaining chickpeas to a fairly smooth purée with the reserved cooking liquid, the oil and lemon juice. Transfer to a bowl.

Place the tomatoes in a bowl and cover with boiling water. Leave for 30 seconds, then peel, deseed and roughly chop. Add the tomatoes to the chickpea purée with the lemon zest, garlic, spring onions. The parsley or mint and seasoning.

Mix well and refrigerate for 30 minutes. Before serving, garnish with the reserved chickpeas and drizzle with a little extra olive oil.

Individual Antipasto Tarts

makes 4

2 eggs

70g (2½oz) plain (all-purpose) white flour, sieved

225g (8oz) jar cranberry and orange sauce, for dipping

vegetable oil, for deep-frying

1 zucchini (courgette), cut into thick slices

1 large red onion, cut into wedges

225g (8oz) broccoli, cut into small florets

1 red capsicum (bell pepper), deseeded and cut into strips

125g (4oz) green beans, topped only

125g (4oz) asparagus, trimmed

sea salt

fresh basil leaves, to garnish

To make the batter, lightly whisk together the eggs and ¼ cup ice-cold water, then pour on to the flour all at once and whisk quickly, until the batter is smooth.

Heat the cranberry and orange sauce in a small saucepan, over a gentle heat, until warm and runny. Remove from the heat and place in a bowl.

Heat 5cm of oil in a wok or frying pan. Dip the vegetables into the batter and coat well. Test the temperature of the oil by dropping in a little batter, if it floats straight back to the surface the oil is hot enough.

Deep-fry the vegetables in small batches for 3–4 minutes or until crisp and golden. Remove with a slotted spoon and drain on absorbent paper. Season with salt. Deep-fry the basil leaves for 20 seconds, until crisp. Serve the vegetables immediately with the cranberry and orange sauce.

Mushrooms on Herbed Muffins

serves 6

500g (1lb) mixed mushrooms, including wild, oyster and shiitake

2 tablespoons olive oil

salt and black pepper

25g (¾oz) butter

1 clove garlic, crushed

3 tablespoons fresh parsley, chopped

3 tablespoons chives, chopped plus extra whole chives to garnish

2 teaspoons sherry vinegar or balsamic vinegar

4 tablespoons soft cheese

3 English white muffins

Halve any large mushrooms. Heat 2 teaspoons of the oil in a heavy-based frying pan, then add all the mushrooms, season lightly and fry over a medium to high heat for 5 minutes or until they start to release their juices.

Remove the mushrooms and drain on absorbent paper, then set aside. Add the rest of the oil and half the butter to the pan and heat until the butter melts. Add the garlic and stir for 1 minute.

Return the mushrooms to the pan, then increase the heat to high and fry for 5 minutes or until they are tender and starting to crisp. Stir in the remaining butter and 2 tablespoons each of parsley and chives, drizzle with the vinegar and season.

Mix the soft cheese with the remaining parsley and chives. Split and toast the muffins. Spread the soft cheese mixture over the muffin halves and place on serving plates. Top with the mushrooms and garnish with the whole chives

Three Kinds of Deep-fried Tofu

serves 4

1 block tofu, cut into 12 squares

arrowroot

3 teaspoons seaweed powder

3 teaspoons black sesame seeds

400mL (14fl oz) udonji

chives

Lightly roll tofu cubes in arrowroot. Deep-fry tofu for 3–4 minutes.

Roll 4 cubes in seaweed powder to coat and roll 4 cubes in black sesame seeds.

Place one seaweed, one black sesame seed and one plain tofu cube in each serving bowl.

Pour 100mL (3½fl oz) of udonji into each bowl. Garnish with chives and serve.

Chilli Bean Potatoes

serves 4

4 potatoes, scrubbed

3 large red chillies

1 tablespoon tomato paste

½ teaspoon paprika

315g (11⅛oz) canned red kidney
   beans, drained and rinsed

freshly ground black pepper

½ cup tasty cheese, grated

Preheat the oven to 220°C (420°F). Bake the potatoes and chillies for 50 minutes until potatoes are soft. Remove from oven and allow to cool slightly. Remove the skins and seeds from the chillies, then set aside.

Cut tops from potatoes and scoop out flesh, leaving a thin shell. Place potato flesh, tomato paste, paprika and roasted chilli in a bowl and mash. Stir in beans and season to taste with black pepper.

Spoon mixture into potato shells, top with cheese, and bake for 10–15 minutes or until heated through and lightly browned.

Note For a speedier version of this dish you can microwave the potatoes on high (100%) for 10 minutes or until tender, rather than baking them. Allow the potatoes to stand for at least 10 minutes before cutting and removing the flesh.

Pickled Tomato and Beans

serves 4

2 tablespoons olive oil

1 clove garlic, crushed

1 tablespoon chopped fresh basil

315g (11⅛oz) canned three-bean
mix, drained and rinsed

250g (9oz) cherry tomatoes,
halved

1 tablespoon white vinegar

½ teaspoon sugar

Heat oil in a large frying pan, add garlic and basil and cook for 1 minute. Stir in beans and tomatoes, cover and cook for 5–6 minutes.

Add vinegar and sugar and cook for 2 minutes longer or until heated through. Serve immediately.

Note This recipe uses canned three-bean mix, which is a mixture of butter beans, red kidney beans and lima beans. Any canned mixed beans can be used.

Grilled Vegetable Bruschetta

serves 4

1 red or yellow capsicum (bell pepper), deseeded and sliced into strips

1 zucchini (courgette), halved and thinly sliced lengthwise

1 red onion, thinly sliced

2 large Roma tomatoes, thickly sliced

3 tablespoons extra virgin olive oil

2 teaspoons wholegrain mustard

black pepper

1 ciabatta loaf, cut into 8 slices, or 8 slices from a baguette

1 clove garlic, halved

8 pitted black olives, thinly sliced

fresh basil to garnish

Preheat the grill to high and line the grill rack with foil. Place the capsicum, zucchini, onion and tomatoes in a bowl. Whisk together 2 tablespoons of oil, the mustard and black pepper, then pour over the vegetables and toss gently to coat.

Spread the vegetables in a single layer on the grill rack and grill for 3–4 minutes on each side, until lightly browned. Set aside and keep warm.

Toast the bread slices on both sides under the grill and, while still hot, rub the garlic halves over one side of each piece of toast. Divide the vegetables between the toast slices, piling them onto the garlic side. Scatter over the olives and drizzle over the remaining oil. Garnish with fresh basil and serve.

Bubble and Squeak with Chutney

serves 6

675g (1lb 7oz) potatoes, peeled and cut into even-sized pieces

1 clove garlic, peeled

125g (4oz) Savoy cabbage, finely shredded

4 spring onions, finely sliced

sea salt and freshly ground black pepper

25g (¾oz) butter

1 tablespoon sunflower oil

CHUTNEY

2 large red onions, or 6 small red onions, finely chopped

50g (1¾oz) brown sugar

1 tablespoon white wine vinegar

Place the potatoes and garlic in a saucepan and cover with water. Bring to the boil, cover and simmer for 15–20 minutes, until tender. Drain, return to the pan and mash until smooth. Cool.

Meanwhile, place the cabbage in a saucepan and pour over boiling water to just cover, bring back to the boil, then drain. Add the cabbage, spring onions and seasoning to the potato and mix well.

Place all the ingredients for the chutney in a saucepan and bring to the boil over a low heat. Simmer gently, uncovered, for about 20 minutes or until almost all of the liquid has evaporated.

Divide the potato into eight and shape into flat rounds. Melt the butter and oil in a frying pan and fry the cakes over a medium heat for 5 minutes on one side. Turn over, taking care as the cakes are quite soft, and cook for a further 5 minutes, until golden and heated through. Serve with the chutney.

Watercress Roulade with Parmesan

serves 4

20g (⅔oz) Parmesan cheese, grated

85g (3oz) watercress, finely chopped, thick stems discarded

4 medium eggs, beaten

salt and black pepper

FILLING

200g (7oz) soft cheese, at room temperature

3 tablespoons milk

85g (3oz) watercress, finely chopped and thick stems discarded, with a few sprigs reserved to garnish

5 spring onions, finely chopped

salt and pepper

Preheat the oven to 200°C (400°F). Lightly oil a 23 x 30cm (9 x 11in) Swiss roll tin, line with baking paper, then sprinkle with half the Parmesan.

Mix together the watercress and eggs, season, then pour into the tin. Cook for 7–8 minutes, until the eggs have set. Remove from the oven and leave to cool for 5 minutes. Sprinkle over the remaining Parmesan. Lay a sheet of baking paper over the top and set aside for 35 minutes or until completely cool.

To make the filling, mix the soft cheese with the milk, watercress, onions and seasoning. Turn the cooled roulade onto a chopping board. Peel off the top sheet of paper, then spread the filling over the base. Roll up from the short end, peeling off the paper as you go. Refrigerate for 30 minutes, then serve in slices, garnished with watercress.

Red Onion and Chilli Tarts

serves 4

375g (13oz) ready-rolled puff
  pastry

1 tablespoon olive oil

200g (7oz) red onions, halved and
  finely sliced lengthwise

1 small red chilli, deseeded and
  thinly sliced

salt and black pepper

2 tablespoons red pesto

25g (¾oz) pine nuts

Preheat the oven to 220°C (420°F). Open out the pastry sheet and cut out 4 x 12cm (1½ x 7¾in) rounds. Use a slightly smaller cutter or a sharp knife to score a 1cm (⅓in) border on each—this will form the rim. Place the rounds on a baking sheet.

Heat the oil in a large frying pan. Fry the onions for 10 minutes or until softened, stirring. Add the chilli and cook gently for 1 minute, then season.

Spread the pesto over the pastry rounds, leaving the rim clear. Spoon the onion mixture over the pesto and scatter with the pine nuts. Cook for 12–15 minutes, until the pastry has risen and is golden brown.

Green Vegetable Terrine with Salsa

serves 6

100g (3½oz) peas

100g (3½oz) broad beans

125g (4oz) thin asparagus spears,
   cut into 1cm (⅓in) pieces

2 Savoy cabbage leaves, sliced

sunflower oil for greasing

4 large eggs

1 clove garlic, crushed

2 teaspoons ground coriander

350g (12oz) ricotta cheese

6 tablespoons coconut milk

3 tablespoons thickened cream

1 tablespoon fresh coriander
   (cilantro), chopped

1 tablespoon fresh basil, chopped
   plus extra to garnish

salt and black pepper

SALSA

3 tomatoes

1 ripe avocado, chopped

grated zest and juice of 1 lime

2 French shallots, finely chopped

1 clove garlic, crushed

1 chilli, deseeded and chopped

Bring a saucepan of lightly salted water to the boil. Cook the peas, broad beans, asparagus and cabbage for 3 minutes to soften, then refresh under cold running water, drain and set aside.

Preheat the oven to 180°C (350°F). Grease a 450g (15oz) loaf tin with the oil, line with baking paper and grease again. Whisk the eggs until foamy, then whisk in the garlic, ground coriander, ricotta, coconut milk and cream. Stir in the vegetables, then add the fresh coriander and basil. Season, then pour the mixture into the tin.

Place the loaf tin on a double layer of newspaper in a roasting tin. Pour boiling water into the roasting tin to reach halfway up the loaf tin. Cook for 50–55 minutes, until firm. Cool for 1½ hours, then remove from the roasting tin, cover with foil and refrigerate for 2 hours or overnight.

Meanwhile, make the salsa. Put the tomatoes in a bowl, cover with boiling water and leave for 30 seconds. Remove, peel and deseed, then chop. Mix the tomatoes with the avocado, lime zest and juice, shallots, garlic and chilli, then season. Turn out the terrine, garnish with basil and serve with the salsa

side dishes

Baked Onions and Green Peppers

serves 6

4 onions, quartered

3 sprigs of thyme

100mL (3½fl oz) vegetable stock
or white wine

3 tablespoons cider vinegar

2 tablespoons olive oil

1 tablespoon molasses or soft
dark brown sugar

2 teaspoons caraway seeds

4 cloves garlic, peeled and left
whole

salt and black pepper

3 green capsicums (bell peppers),
deseeded and cut into wide
strips

Preheat the oven to 200°C (400°F). Place the onions, thyme, stock or wine, vinegar, oil, molasses or sugar, caraway seeds and garlic in an ovenproof dish. Season, cover with foil and bake for 30 minutes or until the onions have softened slightly.

Remove the foil, baste the onions with the cooking liquid, then re-cover and return to the oven for 30 minutes or until the onions are just tender. Add a little water if the liquid has evaporated.

Increase the oven heat to 250°C (485°F). Remove the foil from the dish and stir in the capsicum strips. Return the dish to the oven, uncovered, and cook the vegetables for 8–10 minutes, turning halfway through cooking, until most of the liquid has evaporated and the vegetables have started to brown.

Eggplant (Aubergine) Rolls

serves 4

2 eggplants (aubergine), about 225g (8oz)

3 tablespoons olive oil

3 medium tomatoes, deseeded and diced

150g (5oz) mozzarella cheese, finely diced

2 tablespoons fresh basil, chopped

salt and freshly ground black pepper

fresh basil leaves, for serving

DRESSING

¼ cup olive oil

1 tomato, diced

1 tablespoon balsamic vinegar

2 tablespoons pine nuts, toasted

Remove the stalks from eggplants, and thinly slice the eggplants lengthwise to 5mm (¹/₈in) thick. Brush the slices on both sides with oil, and grill on both sides (until soft and beginning to brown).

Preheat the oven to 180°C (350°F). Combine together (in a bowl) the tomatoes, mozzarella, basil, and seasoning. Spoon a little onto the end of each slice of eggplant, and roll up. Place seam-side down in a greased ovenproof dish, bake for 15–17 minutes.

To make the dressing, sauté the tomato until softened in a little of the oil. Add the remaining oil, balsamic vinegar and pine nuts, and gently warm. Season to taste. Arrange the rolls on a platter, and spoon the dressing over the rolls.

Garnish with fresh basil leaves to serve.

Spicy Green Salad

serves 20

salt and black pepper

1kg (2lb 3oz) mixture of broccoli florets, peas, snowpeas, broad beans, asparagus and fine green beans

400g (14oz) canned chickpeas, drained

1 romaine lettuce, cut into ribbons

85g (3oz) watercress, thick stalks discarded

1 avocado, thickly sliced

2 tablespoons fresh mixed herbs, such as flat-leaf parsley and coriander (cilantro), finely chopped

DRESSING

2 tablespoons sesame oil

150mL (5fl oz) sunflower oil

4 spring onions, finely chopped

2 cloves garlic, crushed

1 teaspoon dried crushed chillies

2 teaspoons ground coriander

2 teaspoons ground ginger

juice of 2 lemons

To make the dressing, heat the sesame oil and 75mL (2½fl oz) of the sunflower oil in a frying pan, then fry the spring onions and garlic for 1–2 minutes, until soft but not coloured. Add the crushed chillies, coriander and ginger and stir-fry for 2–3 minutes to release the flavours, then transfer to a bowl.

Bring a large saucepan of salted water to the boil. Add the vegetables and simmer for 3–4 minutes, until cooked but still crunchy. Drain.

In a large bowl, mix the vegetables with the chickpeas. Pour over the spicy dressing, stir, then drizzle over half the lemon juice and half the remaining sunflower oil. Stir again and season if necessary. Cover and set aside until needed.

Toss the lettuce with the watercress. Season, drizzle with a little lemon juice and oil, then toss lightly. Arrange with the vegetables in a serving bowl. Brush the avocado with lemon juice to stop it browning, then add to the salad with the herbs. Drizzle over the remaining lemon juice and oil. Season to taste.

Creamy Polenta and Spinach Bake

serves 4

1 tablespoon olive oil

1 small onion, finely chopped

2 cloves garlic, crushed

½ teaspoon ground coriander

750g (1lb 10oz) fresh spinach

1 cup thickened cream

50g (1¾oz) Gorgonzola, crumbled

pinch of ground nutmeg

salt and black pepper

500g (1lb) ready-made polenta, thinly sliced

150g (5oz) mozzarella ball, thinly sliced

Preheat the oven to 230°C (450°F). Heat the oil in a saucepan and gently fry the onion, garlic and coriander for
5 minutes or until the onion is softened.

Blanch the spinach in boiling salted water for 1 minute, refresh under cold running water, then drain well and squeeze out any excess moisture. Stir the spinach into the pan with the cream, Gorgonzola, nutmeg, salt and pepper. Bring to a simmer, then transfer to a large, shallow, ovenproof dish.

Arrange the polenta and mozzarella slices over the top of the spinach mixture, pressing down well. Bake for 15 minutes or until bubbling. Meanwhile, preheat the grill to high. Place the bake under the grill for 1–2 minutes, until browned.

Carrots and Snowpeas with Sesame Seeds

serves 4

½ cucumber

2 tablespoons sesame seeds

1 tablespoon sunflower oil

4 carrots, cut into matchsticks

225g (8oz) snowpeas

6 spring onions, chopped

1 tablespoon lemon juice

black pepper

Peel the cucumber, cut it in half lengthwise and scoop out the seeds. Slice into half moons.

Heat a non-stick wok or large frying pan. Add the sesame seeds and dry-fry for 1 minute or until toasted, tossing constantly. Remove and set aside. Add the oil, then the cucumber and carrots and stir-fry over a high heat for 2 minutes. Add the snowpeas and spring onions and stir-fry for a further 2–3 minutes, until all the vegetables are cooked but still crisp.

Sprinkle over the lemon juice and sesame seeds, toss to mix and stir-fry for a few seconds to heat through. Season with pepper and serve.

Roasted Shallots with Rosemary

serves 4

600g (1lb 5oz) shallots or pickling
  onions

2 tablespoons olive oil

1–2 tablespoons fresh rosemary,
  chopped

black pepper

Preheat the oven to 200°C (400°F). Place the shallots in a roasting tin, drizzle over the oil, sprinkle with the rosemary and black pepper, then toss to mix well.

Cook in the oven, stirring once or twice for 30–40 minutes, until the shallots are tender and golden brown. Serve hot

Spinach with Sesame Seeds

serves 6

750g (1lb 10oz) fresh spinach,
stalks removed

1 tablespoon peanut oil

1 teaspoon sesame oil

3 cloves garlic, chopped

2 tablespoons sesame seeds

juice of ½ lemon and ¼ teaspoon
finely grated lemon zest
(optional)

salt and black pepper

Place the spinach in a large bowl, cover with boiling water, then leave for 2–3 minutes. Drain, then refresh under cold running water. Squeeze out any excess water, then coarsely chop.

Heat the peanut and sesame oil in a wok or large, heavy-based frying pan. Add the garlic and the sesame seeds and fry for 1–2 minutes, until the garlic has begun to brown and the seeds have started to pop.

Stir in the spinach and fry for 1–2 minutes, until heated through. Add the lemon juice and zest (if using), season and mix well.

Asparagus with Lemon Sauce

serves 4

2 bundles asparagus, about 550g
(19½oz) in total

salt and black pepper

SAUCE

2 medium eggs

2 tablespoons pickled cucumber
or gherkins, chopped

1 teaspoon capers, rinsed, dried
and chopped

1 teaspoon Dijon mustard

5 tablespoons olive oil

finely grated zest and juice of
½ lemon

pinch of caster (superfine) sugar
(optional)

2 tablespoons fresh parsley, finely
chopped

2 tablespoons crème fraîche or
fromage frais

First make the sauce. Place the eggs in a pan of cold water, bring to the boil and cook for 10 minutes or until hard-boiled. Peel, halve and remove the yolks, discarding the whites.

Mash the yolks in a bowl with the cucumber or gherkins. Stir in the capers and mustard, then gradually beat in the oil. Alternatively, blend in a food processor or with a hand blender. Beat in the lemon zest, juice and sugar, if using, then stir in the parsley and crème fraîche or fromage frais.

Cut the tough ends off the asparagus, then peel the lower 5cm (2in) using a vegetable peeler. Fill a saucepan with water to a depth of about 4cm, add a little salt, then bring to the boil. Stand the asparagus spears in the pan, keeping the tips out of the water. Simmer for 5–6 minutes, until just tender, then drain. Serve the asparagus with the sauce and grind over black pepper.

Fragrant Pilaf Rice

serves 4

large pinch of saffron strands

225g (8oz) basmati rice

25g (¾oz) butter

1 French shallot, finely chopped

3 cardamom pods

1 cinnamon stick

salt

Briefly grind the saffron using a pestle and mortar, then mix the powder with 1 tablespoon of boiling water and set aside. Rinse the rice and drain.

Melt the butter in a large, heavy-based saucepan. Fry the shallot gently for 2 minutes or until softened. Add the cardamom pods, cinnamon and rice and mix well.

Add 300mL (10½fl oz) of water, the saffron mixture and salt. Bring to the boil, then reduce the heat and cover the pan tightly. Simmer the rice for 15 minutes or until the liquid has been absorbed and the rice is tender. Remove the cardamom pods and cinnamon stick before serving.

Pumpkin with Lemon and Cheese Sauce

serves 6

750g (1lb 10oz) pumpkin or squash, peeled, deseeded and cut into chunks

200mL (7fl oz) vegetable stock

2 teaspoons arrowroot

grated zest of ½ lemon and juice of 1 lemon

150g (5oz) aged Cheddar, grated

2 tablespoons fresh dill or parsley, chopped

salt and black pepper

Place the pumpkin or squash in a steamer or in a metal colander covered with foil. Set over a saucepan of simmering water and steam for 5–10 minutes, until tender but still firm.

Meanwhile, bring the stock to the boil in a small saucepan. Mix the arrowroot with the lemon juice until smooth, then stir in the lemon zest and add to the boiling stock. Simmer, stirring constantly, for 1–2 minutes, until the sauce thickens and looks glossy. Add 125g (4oz) of the Cheddar and simmer for a further 1–2 minutes, until the cheese has melted. Stir in the dill or parsley, season, and mix well.

Preheat the grill to high. Transfer the pumpkin to a flameproof dish, pour over the lemon sauce and sprinkle with the reserved Cheddar. Place under the grill and cook for 5–8 minutes, until the sauce is bubbling and golden.

Zucchini (Courgette) Polenta Slices

serves 4

15g (½oz) butter

3 tablespoons olive oil

250g (9oz) zucchini (courgette), grated

3 cups vegetable stock

175g (6oz) instant polenta

salt and black pepper

40g (1½oz) Parmesan, finely grated

Lightly butter a shallow 22cm (8½in) square roasting tin. Heat the butter and 1 tablespoon of the oil in a large frying pan. Fry the zucchini for 3–4 minutes, stirring frequently, until softened but not browned. Remove from the heat.

Bring the stock to the boil in a large saucepan. Sprinkle in the polenta, stirring with a wooden spoon, and continue to stir for 5 minutes or until the polenta thickens and begins to come away from the sides of the pan. Remove from the heat and stir in the zucchini. Season to taste.

Tip the polenta into the roasting tin, spreading evenly, then sprinkle with Parmesan and leave for 1 hour to cool and set.

Heat a ridged cast-iron grill pan over a high heat. Cut the polenta into slices, brush with the rest of the oil and cook for 2–4 minutes on each side, until golden. Alternatively, cook under a preheated grill.

Pak Choy in Oyster Sauce

serves 4

400g (14oz) pak choy

3 tablespoons oyster sauce (see note)

1 tablespoon peanut oil

salt

Trim the ends of the pak choy stalks, then separate the leaves and rinse thoroughly. Mix together the oyster sauce and oil.

Put the pak choy into a large saucepan of lightly salted boiling water and cook, uncovered, for 3 minutes or until tender. Drain thoroughly, return the pak choy to the pan, then add the oyster sauce and oil mixture and toss to coat evenly.

Note Check labels carefully, vegetarian-style oyster sauce is available although not common.

Spicy Cauliflower with Garlic

serves 4

2 slices brown bread

1 cauliflower, cut into florets

salt and black pepper

4 tablespoons olive oil

1 clove garlic, crushed

1 red chilli, finely chopped

8 black olives, pitted and halved

1 tablespoon capers

Preheat the oven to 160°C (325°F). Place the bread in the oven for 20 minutes or until it dries out and becomes crisp. Process in a food processor to make breadcrumbs. Alternatively, use a grater.

Place the cauliflower in a saucepan, cover with boiling water and add a little salt. Return to the boil, simmer for 1 minute or until slightly softened, then drain well.

Heat the oil in a large, heavy-based frying pan. Add the garlic, chilli and cauliflower and fry for 3 minutes or until the cauliflower starts to brown. Add the olives, capers, breadcrumbs and seasoning. Fry for a further 1 minute or until the breadcrumbs soak up the oil and flavour.

soups

Roma Tomato, Lentil and Basil Soup

serves 4

75g (2½oz) continental lentils

1kg (2lb 3oz) Roma tomatoes

1 tablespoon olive oil

2 onions, chopped

2 tablespoons sun-dried tomato purée

750mL (24fl oz) vegetable stock

1 bay leaf

black pepper

3 tablespoons fresh basil, chopped, plus extra leaves to garnish

Rinse the lentils, drain, then add to a large saucepan of boiling water. Simmer, covered, for 25 minutes or until tender. Drain, rinse and set aside.

Meanwhile, place the tomatoes in a bowl, cover with boiling water, leave for 30 seconds, then drain. Remove the skins, deseed and chop. Heat the oil in a large saucepan, add the onions and cook for 10 minutes or until softened, stirring occasionally. Stir in the tomatoes, tomato purée, stock, bay leaf and black pepper. Bring to the boil and simmer, covered, stirring occasionally, for 25 minutes or until all the vegetables are cooked.

Remove the pan from the heat and cool for a few minutes. Remove and discard the bay leaf, then purée the soup until smooth in a food processor, liquidiser, or with a hand blender. Return to a clean pan, stir in the lentils and chopped basil, then reheat gently. Serve garnished with fresh basil.

Watercress Soup

serves 4

1 tablespoon sunflower oil

4 French shallots, finely chopped

1 leek, thinly sliced

225g (8oz) potatoes, diced

225g (8oz) watercress, chopped

450mL (15fl oz) vegetable stock

450mL (15fl oz) milk

black pepper

Heat the oil in a large saucepan, then add the shallots and leek and cook gently for 5 minutes or until softened, stirring occasionally. Add the potatoes and watercress to the shallot mixture and cook, stirring occasionally for a further 3 minutes or until the watercress wilts.

Stir in the stock, milk and black pepper. Bring to the boil, then reduce the heat and simmer, covered but stirring occasionally, for 20 minutes or until the potatoes are cooked and tender.

Remove the pan from the heat and cool for a few minutes. Purée the soup until smooth in a food processor, liquidiser, or with a hand blender. Return to a clean pan and reheat gently, until piping hot. Serve seasoned with coarsely ground black pepper.

Coconut, Sweet Potato and Spinach Soup

serves 4

25g (¾oz) butter

450g (15oz) sweet potatoes, cut into 1cm (⅓in) dice

1 onion, chopped

2 cloves garlic, crushed

1 teaspoon grated root ginger

1 tablespoon medium curry paste

600mL (20fl oz) vegetable stock

200mL (7fl oz) coconut milk

juice of 1 lime

¼ teaspoon dried crushed chillies

175g (6oz) fresh spinach, shredded

salt and black pepper

Melt the butter in a saucepan and fry the potatoes, onion, garlic, ginger and curry paste for 5 minutes
or until lightly golden.

Add the stock, coconut milk, lime juice and chilli. Bring to the boil, cover and simmer for 15 minutes or until the potatoes are tender.

Leave the soup to cool a little, then purée half of it with a hand blender. Return the purée to the pan, add the spinach and cook for 1–2 minutes, until the spinach has just wilted and the soup has heated through. Season to taste.

Pea and Fresh Mint Soup

serves 4

50g (1¾oz) butter

bunch of spring onions, chopped

1 mushroom stock cube, crumbled

450g (15oz) shelled fresh peas, or
   frozen peas

2 little gem lettuces, shredded

salt and black pepper

2 tablespoons fresh mint,
   chopped

½ cup thickened single cream

pinch of caster (superfine) sugar
   (optional)

fresh lemon juice (optional)

thickened cream to serve and
   chopped fresh chives to garnish

Melt the butter in a large heavy-based saucepan. Add the spring onions, stock cube, cover and cook gently for 2 minutes.

Add the peas and lettuce and 900mL (30½fl oz) of water. Season well, bring to the boil, then simmer for 10 minutes or until the vegetables are tender. Purée with the mint and cream until smooth, using a food processor or a hand blender.

Return the soup to the pan. Season again, if necessary, then add the caster sugar and lemon juice, if using. Reheat gently but do not allow the soup to boil. Serve in bowls with a spoonful of cream drizzled on top and a sprinkling of chives.

Roasted Peppers and Tomato Soup

serves 4

3 red or orange capsicums (bell peppers), halved and deseeded

1 onion, unpeeled and halved

4 large Roma tomatoes

4 cloves garlic, unpeeled

350mL (12fl oz) vegetable stock

1 tablespoon tomato purée

salt and black pepper

2 tablespoons fresh parsley, chopped

Preheat the oven to 200°C (400°F). Place the capsicums and onion on a baking sheet, cut-side down, and add the whole tomatoes and garlic. Cook in the oven for 30 minutes or until tender and well browned.

Leave the vegetables and garlic to cool for 10 minutes, then peel them. Place the vegetables and garlic in a food processor with half the stock and blend until smooth. Alternatively use a hand blender.

Return to the pan, add the remaining stock and the tomato purée, then bring to the boil. Season to taste and scatter with parsley just before serving.

Spinach Soup with Cheese Toasts

serves 6

2 tablespoons olive oil

25g (¾oz) butter

250g (9oz) floury potatoes, such as King Edward, peeled and cut into 2.5cm (1in) cubes

250g (9oz) spinach leaves

1 teaspoon freshly grated nutmeg

6 cups vegetable stock

salt and black pepper

4 tablespoons crème fraîche

100g (3½oz) Gruyère, Caerphilly or Cheddar cheese, grated

1 large egg, beaten

day-old narrow baguette, cut diagonally into 18 x 1cm (⅓in) slices

Heat the oil and half the butter in a large saucepan. Fry the potatoes for 1 minute, then add the spinach and the nutmeg. Cook for 2 minutes or until the spinach is wilting.

Add the stock to the potato and spinach mixture, season lightly and bring to the boil. Reduce the heat, cover and simmer for 10–15 minutes, until the potatoes are tender. Leave to cool for 10 minutes.

Pour the soup into a food processor and blend until smooth. Alternatively, use a hand blender. Stir in half the crème fraîche, then adjust the seasoning to taste. Set aside.

Preheat the grill. Mix the grated cheese with the egg and the rest of the crème fraîche. Lightly toast the bread slices, then spread the cheese mixture over one side of each slice. Dot with the rest of the butter and season with a little black pepper. Grill for 5 minutes or until bubbling and golden. Heat the soup through and serve topped with the cheese toasts.

Indian-Spiced Potato and Onion Soup

serves 4

1 tablespoon vegetable oil

1 onion, finely chopped

1cm (⅓in) piece root ginger, finely chopped

2 large potatoes, cut into 1cm (⅓in) cubes

2 teaspoons ground cumin

2 teaspoons ground coriander

½ teaspoon turmeric

1 teaspoon ground cinnamon

4 cups vegetable stock

salt and black pepper

1 tablespoons natural yoghurt to garnish

Heat the oil in a large saucepan. Fry the onion and ginger for 5 minutes or until softened. Add the potatoes and fry for another minute, stirring often.

Mix the cumin, coriander, turmeric and cinnamon with 2 tablespoons of cold water to make a paste. Add to the onion and potato, stirring well, and fry for 1 minute to release the flavours.

Add the stock and season to taste. Bring to the boil, then reduce the heat, cover and simmer for 30 minutes or until the potato is tender. Blend until smooth in a food processor or press through a metal sieve. Return to the pan and gently heat through. Garnish with the yogurt and more black pepper.

Provençal-style Soup with Onion Pesto

serves 4

2 tablespoons extra virgin
  olive oil

1 onion, chopped

1 medium potato, peeled and
  chopped

1 carrot, chopped

1 yellow capsicum (bell pepper),
  deseeded and chopped

500mL (17½fl oz) garlic and herb
  stock, made from 1½ stock
  cubes

2 sticks celery, chopped

2 zucchini (courgette), chopped

400g (14oz) canned chopped
  tomatoes

1 tablespoon tomato purée

sea salt

freshly ground black pepper

PESTO

6 spring onions, roughly chopped,
  including green part

50g (1¾oz) Parmesan cheese,
  grated

4 tablespoons extra virgin
  olive oil

For the soup, heat the oil in a large heavy-based saucepan, then add the onion, potato, carrot and yellow capsicum. Cook uncovered for 5 minutes over a medium heat, stirring occasionally, until the vegetables just start to brown.

Add the stock, celery and zucchini and bring to the boil. Cover and simmer for 10 minutes or until the vegetables are tender. Stir in the tomatoes and tomato purée, and season generously. Simmer uncovered for 10 minutes.

Meanwhile, make the pesto. Place the spring onions, Parmesan and oil in a food processor and purée to a fairly smooth paste. Ladle the soup into bowls and top with a spoonful of the pesto.

French Vegetables with Pistou

serves 4-6

500g (1lb) fresh borlotti or dried
   haricot beans

1 large onion

500g (1lb) green beans

500g (1lb) baby squash

6 medium potatoes

30g (1oz) butter

1–2 teaspoon salt

60g (2oz) farfalle (pasta bows)

PISTOU

1 cup basil leaves

4 cloves garlic

1 large tomato

1 tablespoon tomato paste

½ cup grated Parmesan or Gruyère
   cheese

3 tablespoons olive oil

If using dried beans, soak overnight. Place soaked and drained dried beans in a pan with fresh water to cover. Bring to the boil, cover and simmer gently for 15 minutes. Drain.

Chop onion finely. Trim green beans and cut into short lengths. Cut squash into 5mm slices. Peel potatoes and cut into 1cm (⅓in) dice. Melt butter in a large deep pan and sauté prepared vegetables (including dried and cooked or fresh white beans) until softened (about 5 minutes). Cover with cold water and add salt. Cover and simmer gently for 1 hour. Add farfalle to soup, cooking for a further 15 minutes.

Make pistou by processing the basil leaves with the garlic in a food processor or blender. Peel and chop the tomato and add to the basil with the tomato paste and grated cheese. Purée to a paste, adding oil gradually. Stir the pistou into the soup just before serving. Serve piping hot with crusty bread.

Chilled Yoghurt Soup

serves 4-6

1 large telegraph cucumber

1 cup thickened cream

200mL (7fl oz) natural yoghurt

2 tablespoons white wine vinegar

1 tablespoon balsamic vinegar

2 tablespoons fresh mint, chopped

1 clove garlic, crushed

salt and freshly ground black pepper

extra mint and slices of cucumber, to garnish

Peel and grate the cucumber.

Combine the cream, yoghurt and vinegars together, and whisk lightly, until smooth. Stir in the cucumber, mint, garlic and seasoning. Cover and refrigerate for three hours.

Stir and taste for seasoning before serving chilled. Garnish with a slice of cucumber, a sprig of mint and cracked pepper.

Thick Minestrone with Pesto

serves 4

3 tablespoons olive oil

1 onion, chopped

2 cloves garlic, chopped

1 potato, cut into 1cm (⅓in) cubes

2 small carrots, cut into 1cm (⅓in) cubes

1 large zucchini (courgette), cut into 1cm (⅓in) cubes

¼ white cabbage, chopped

700mL (24fl oz) vegetable stock

800g (28fl oz) canned chopped tomatoes

75g (2½oz) pasta shapes, such as shells (conchiglie)

salt and black pepper

4 tablespoons grated Parmesan

4 tablespoons pesto

Place the oil in a large heavy-based saucepan, then add the onion, garlic, potato, carrots, zucchini and cabbage and cook for 5–7 minutes, until slightly softened.

Add the stock and tomatoes and bring to the boil. Reduce the heat and simmer for 20 minutes, then add the pasta shapes and seasoning and cook for a further 15 minutes or until the pasta is tender but still firm to the bite. Divide the soup between bowls and top each serving with a tablespoon of Parmesan and pesto.

Curried Cream of Vegetable Soup

serves 4

3 tablespoons vegetable oil

2 tablespoons curry powder

pinch each of ground cinnamon, nutmeg, turmeric and ginger

3 carrots, diced

2 onions, chopped

2 cloves garlic, chopped

2 potatoes, diced

2 zucchini (courgette), diced

4 cups vegetable stock

300g (10½oz) canned cannellini beans, drained

220g (7¾oz) canned red kidney beans, drained

200mL (7fl oz) crème fraîche

salt

2 teaspoons fresh flat-leaf parsley, chopped

Place the oil in a large heavy-based saucepan. Add the curry powder, cinnamon, nutmeg, turmeric and ginger and cook for 1 minute, then add the carrots, onions, garlic, potatoes and zucchini. Stir to coat thoroughly in the oil and spice mixture, and cook for a further 5 minutes.

Add the stock and bring to the boil. Reduce the heat and simmer for 20 minutes or until the vegetables are tender. Add the cannellini and red kidney beans and gently heat through. Remove from the heat and stir in the crème fraîche. Season to taste and serve sprinkled with the parsley.

Almond Soup

serves 4

200g (7oz) almonds

1 clove garlic, peeled

1 tablespoon parsley, finely chopped

8 slices stale bread, preferably brown

⅓ cup olive oil

1 teaspoon ground cumin

⅓ teaspoon saffron threads

4 cups vegetable stock

1 cup milk

salt and pepper

Fry the almonds, garlic, parsley and four slices of the bread in about ¾ of the oil. When golden, put the contents of the pan in a processor and liquidise with the cumin, saffron and a little of the stock. Put in a saucepan, pour in the remaining stock and the milk, season with salt and pepper, and bring to the boil. Lower the heat and cook slowly for about 15 minutes.

Meanwhile, fry the remaining bread slices in the remaining olive oil until golden and crisp.

Bring the soup to the boil again and add the four slices of fried bread. Cover, remove from the stove, and leave for 5 minutes before serving.

Tuscan Bean and Bread Soup

serves 4

½ loaf ciabatta

3 tablespoons olive oil

3 onions, chopped

3 cloves garlic, chopped

800g (1lb 12oz) canned chopped
 tomatoes

400g (14oz) canned flageolet
 beans

600mL (21fl oz) vegetable stock

salt and black pepper

fresh basil to garnish

Preheat the oven to 150°C (300°F). Cut the ciabatta into dice, then place in the oven for 10 minutes to dry out.

Heat the olive oil in a large saucepan, add the onions and garlic, and cook for 3–4 minutes, until soft. Add the tomatoes, beans and stock, bring to the boil, then simmer for 2 minutes.

Stir in the diced ciabatta, bring the soup back to the boil, then simmer for a further 5 minutes. Season, then serve garnished with basil.

Cabbage Parcels in Soup

serves 6

24 cabbage leaves

6 spring onions

½ cup coriander (cilantro), finely chopped

½ cup tofu, crumbled

1 tablespoon light soy sauce

black pepper

6¼ cups vegetable stock

Blanch cabbage leaves in boiling water and cut away any tough sections from their bases.

Cut white ends from spring onions and finely chop the four white heads. Slice two for garnish. Lengthwise, halve green stalks into strips.

Mix well the chopped spring onions and half of the coriander and tofu and soy. Season with pepper.

Into each cabbage leaf, place a tablespoon of mixture and fold first the leaf base then outer edges over it and roll up. Carefully tie up each roll with a length of green spring onion then place the parcels gently into boiling stock to cook for 6 minutes.

Lift parcels into bowls, pour a cup of stock over each and garnish with remaining sliced spring onions and coriander.

Mixed Bean and Vegetable Soup

serves 4-6

½ cup haricot beans, soaked
overnight

½ cup chickpeas (garbanzo beans),
soaked overnight

3 tablespoons olive oil

1 medium onion, diced

1 clove garlic, crushed

1 leek, white part only, diced

6 cups vegetable stock

2 sticks celery, sliced

1 carrot, diced

2 sprigs fresh thyme, chopped

1 small fennel bulb, grated

2 zucchini (courgette), grated

90g (3oz) broad beans

3 medium tomatoes, peeled,
deseeded and chopped

salt and freshly ground black
pepper

freshly grated Parmesan, for
serving

Drain the haricot beans and chickpeas. Place
in a saucepan, cover with water and bring to
the boil for 15 minutes. Cover and simmer for a
further 30 minutes before draining again.

Heat the oil in a saucepan and add the onion,
garlic and leek. Continue stirring until tender. Add
the stock, haricot beans and chickpeas. Cover,
and simmer for 45 minutes (until tender). Add the
remaining ingredients, reserving the Parmesan,
and simmer for a further 15 minutes.

Taste for seasoning, and serve with freshly grated
Parmesan.

Chickpea and Roasted Tomato Soup

serves 4

500g (1lb) dried chickpeas
(garbanzo beans)

1kg (2lb 3oz) Roma tomatoes

1 bulb garlic

⅓ cup olive oil

salt

2 tablespoons dried oregano

2 leeks, sliced, white part only

4 cups vegetable stock

2 tablespoons tomato paste

salt and pepper

fresh oregano leaves

Soak chickpeas in cold water overnight. Place chickpeas in a saucepan covered with water and bring to the boil, then simmer for approximately one hour until chickpeas are cooked. Drain and set aside.

Preheat the oven to 200°C (400°F). Halve the tomatoes and place them in a baking tray. Cut the top off the garlic bulb and place in the baking tray.

Drizzle with a little olive oil, sprinkle with salt and dried oregano, and roast in the oven for 20–30 minutes.

Place the tomatoes and five peeled garlic cloves (reserve the rest) in a food processor, and purée for one minute.

Heat half the remaining oil and sauté the leeks for 3 minutes. Add the stock, and bring to the boil, then reduce heat to simmer. Add the tomato mixture, tomato paste and the chickpeas, season with salt and pepper, and heat through.

To serve, sprinkle with fresh oregano leaves just before serving.

salads

Marinated Mushrooms

serves 4

350g (12oz) mixed mushrooms, such as shiitake, large open, button and oyster, thickly sliced

100g (3½oz) baby spinach leaves

25g (¾oz) watercress, thick stems discarded

fresh thyme to garnish

DRESSING

3 tablespoons extra virgin olive oil

2 tablespoons unsweetened apple juice

2 teaspoons tarragon white wine vinegar

2 teaspoons Dijon mustard

1 clove garlic, crushed

1 tablespoons mixed chopped fresh herbs; choose from oregano, thyme, chives, basil and parsley

black pepper

To make the dressing, place the oil, apple juice, vinegar, mustard, garlic, herbs and black pepper in a bowl and whisk with a fork to mix thoroughly.

Pour the dressing over the mushrooms and stir well. Cover and place in the refrigerator for 2 hours.

Arrange the spinach and watercress on serving plates. Spoon the mushrooms and a little of the dressing over the top and toss lightly to mix. Garnish with fresh thyme.

Three Bean Rice Salad

serves 4

1 cup brown rice

175g (6oz) frozen baby broad
  beans

400g (14oz) canned black-eye
  beans, drained and rinsed

220g (7¾oz) canned red kidney
  beans, drained and rinsed

1 red capsicum (bell pepper),
  deseeded and cut into pieces

1 bunch spring onions, chopped

fresh coriander (cilantro) to
  garnish

DRESSING

150mL (5fl oz) tomato juice

1 tablespoon olive oil

1 tablespoon white wine vinegar

2 teaspoons Dijon mustard

1 clove garlic, crushed

2 tablespoons fresh coriander
  (cilantro), chopped

black pepper

Combine the rice with 1½ cups water in a
saucepan. Bring to the boil, reduce heat to low,
cover and cook for 15 minutes. Remove pan
from heat, allow to stand covered for 10 minutes.
Meanwhile, cook the baby broad beans in a
saucepan of boiling water for 4–5 minutes, until
tender. Rinse under cold water and drain, then
remove the skins if you want. Rinse the rice under
cold water, drain and place in a salad bowl.

To make the dressing, place the tomato juice,
olive oil, vinegar, mustard, garlic, coriander and
black pepper in a small bowl and whisk together
until thoroughly mixed.

Pour the dressing over the rice and stir to mix
well. Add the broad beans, black-eyed beans,
kidney beans, capsicum and spring onions and
mix well. Cover and refrigerate before serving.
Garnish with fresh coriander.

Tomato and Mozzarella Salad

serves 4

6 Roma tomatoes, sliced

250g (9oz) buffalo mozzarella,
  drained and sliced

2 spring onions, sliced

75g (2½oz) black olives

salt and black pepper

DRESSING

3 tablespoons extra virgin
  olive oil

1 clove garlic, crushed

2 teaspoons balsamic vinegar

2 tablespoons fresh basil, chopped

Arrange the tomatoes, mozzarella, spring onions and olives in layers on serving plates and season.

To make the dressing, heat the oil and garlic in a small saucepan over a very low heat for 2 minutes or until the garlic has softened but not browned. Remove the pan from the heat, add the vinegar and basil, then pour over the salad.

Artichokes Braised in White Wine

serves 4

6 artichokes

50mL (1¾fl oz) olive oil

1 small onion, peeled and finely chopped

2 cloves garlic, peeled and finely sliced

200mL (7fl oz) white wine or dry sherry

salt

freshly grated nutmeg

Remove the stalks and outer leaves from the artichokes and wash well. Cut each one into four pieces.

Heat the oil in a casserole and gently sauté the onion and garlic for about 4 minutes. Add the artichokes and wine and season with salt and nutmeg. Cook gently until done, from 20–40 minutes, depending on size and type of the artichokes. (Test by pulling a leaf; if done it will come away easily.) If the liquid should reduce too much you can add a little water.

Roasted Vegetable Salad

serves 4

3 red onions, quartered

3 potatoes, scrubbed and cut into wedges

2 zucchini (courgette), thickly sliced

2 yellow capsicums (bell peppers), deseeded and thickly sliced

4 tomatoes, halved

2 tablespoons olive oil

sea salt and freshly ground black pepper

Parmesan shavings (optional)

DRESSING

3 tablespoons extra virgin olive oil

2 tablespoons clear honey

1 tablespoon balsamic vinegar

finely grated zest and juice of ½ lemon

Preheat the oven to 200°C (400°F). Place all the vegetables in a shallow roasting tin, drizzle over the olive oil and season. Shake the tray gently to ensure the vegetables are well coated with the oil and seasoning. Bake for about 35 minutes, until the vegetables are really tender and slightly charred at the edges.

Meanwhile, mix all the dressing ingredients together and pour over the roasted vegetables. Toss dressing well and divide onto four plates, then top with the Parmesan shavings, if using.

Beetroot, Pear and Bitter-Leaf Salad

serves 4

50g (1¾oz) walnut pieces

200g (7oz) mixed salad leaves, including radicchio and frisée

225g (8oz) cooked beetroot in natural juices, sliced

2 pears, quartered, cored, sliced

40g (1½oz) Parmesan

fresh chives to garnish

DRESSING

2 tablespoons chopped fresh herbs, including basil, chives, mint and parsley

4 tablespoons walnut oil

2 tablespoons extra virgin olive oil

1 clove garlic, crushed

2 teaspoons red wine vinegar

1 teaspoon clear honey

salt and black pepper

Preheat the grill to high. To make the dressing, using a food processor or hand blender, blend the herbs, walnut oil, olive oil, garlic, vinegar and honey until smooth in a food processor or with a hand blender. Season to taste.

Place the walnuts on a baking sheet and grill for 2–3 minutes, until golden, turning often. Arrange the leaves, beetroot and pear slices on serving plates. Scatter over the walnuts, then shave over thin slivers of Parmesan, using a vegetable peeler. Spoon the dressing over the salad and garnish with whole chives.

Broad Beans with Grilled Haloumi

serves 4

100g (3½oz) haloumi cheese, halved

oil for brushing

250g (9oz) broad beans, fresh or frozen

¼ cup lemon juice

⅓ cup olive oil

salt and ground black pepper

4 rounds pita bread

Preheat griller. Slice haloumi cheese very thinly, then brush with olive oil, and grill until starting to brown.

Place the broad beans and haloumi in a bowl, and add the lemon juice, olive oil, salt and ground black pepper, and serve. Serve with toasted pita bread.

Note If broad beans are large, peel off outer skin.

Zucchini (Courgette) and Hazelnut Salad

serves 6

600g (1lb 5oz) small zucchini (courgette)

2 tablespoons sunflower oil, plus extra for frying

5 tablespoons walnut oil

1 tablespoon white wine vinegar

salt and black pepper

100g (3½oz) whole blanched hazelnuts

170g (6oz) watercress, thick stalks removed

75g (2½oz) fetta, crumbled

Pare the zucchini into lengthwise slivers, using a vegetable peeler. In a bowl, mix together the sunflower oil, walnut oil and vinegar and season. Add half the zucchini slivers to the mixture, toss lightly and set aside.

Brush a large frying pan with a little sunflower oil and heat. Lay the remaining zucchini slivers in the pan and cook for 2 minutes on each side or until lightly charred. Remove, season and set aside. Wipe the pan clean.

Roughly crush the hazelnuts, using a pestle and mortar, or put them in a plastic bag, seal it and crush the hazelnuts with a rolling pin. Place in the frying pan and fry for 1–2 minutes, until golden.

Divide the watercress between serving plates. Spoon some of the marinated zucchini into the centre, reserving some of the marinade. Scatter over half the toasted hazelnuts and the fetta. Arrange the charred zucchini on top, and sprinkle over the rest of the hazelnuts and the reserved marinade.

Tomato and Bread Salad with Pesto

serves 4

1 baguette, cubed

2 tablespoons olive oil

3 large tomatoes, cut into 2.5cm
  (1in) chunks

1 small red onion, thinly sliced

100g (3½oz) fetta, crumbled

handful of fresh basil leaves, torn

DRESSING

3 tablespoons olive oil

1 red chilli, deseeded and finely
  chopped

2 tablespoons red pesto

2 tablespoons red wine vinegar

salt and black pepper

Preheat the grill to high. Toss the bread in the oil to coat evenly and spread out on a baking sheet. Grill for 1–2 minutes, until golden, turning occasionally, then leave to cool for 10 minutes.

Meanwhile, make the dressing. Heat the oil in a small saucepan and fry the chilli, stirring, for 1 minute or until softened but not browned. Remove from the heat, leave to cool slightly, then add the pesto and vinegar. Whisk with a fork and season.

Mix the toasted bread with the tomatoes, onion, and fetta. Scatter the basil over the salad. Spoon over the dressing and toss lightly to combine.

Fetta, Artichoke and Walnut Salad

serves 4-6

1 red capsicum (bell peppers), quartered and seeded

1 tablespoon olive oil

100g (3½oz) walnuts

200g (7oz) baby spinach, washed

200g (7oz) Greek fetta, cubed

300g (10½oz) artichoke hearts, quartered

½ cup black olives, pitted

pita bread, for serving

DRESSING

½ cup extra virgin olive oil

¼ cup lemon juice

2 teaspoons honey

2 teaspoons oregano, chopped

freshly ground black pepper

Preheat grill. Place capsicum under grill, and cook until it turns black on top. Cut into strips and set aside.

In a small jar combine all ingredients for dressing, and shake well.

In a frying pan, heat one tablespoon of olive oil, add walnuts, and cook for 1–2 minutes. In a large salad bowl combine baby spinach, feta, artichoke hearts and olives, drizzle dressing over ingredients, and serve with pita bread.

mains

Tomato, Mustard and Brie Tart

serves 4

175g (6oz) plain (all-purpose)
white flour

sea salt

freshly ground black pepper

75g (2½oz) butter, diced

½ cup milk

2 medium egg yolks

1 clove garlic, crushed

1 tablespoon wholegrain mustard

50g (1¾oz) aged Cheddar, grated

4 ripe tomatoes, sliced

125g (4oz) Dutch Brie, thinly
sliced

HERB OIL

1 tablespoon fresh basil, finely
shredded

1 tablespoon fresh parsley, finely
chopped

1 tablespoon fresh coriander
(cilantro), finely chopped

2 tablespoons extra virgin
olive oil

Sift the flour and a pinch of sea salt into a bowl, then rub the butter in, using your fingertips, until it resembles fine breadcrumbs. Add 2 tablespoons of cold water and mix to a dough. Cover and refrigerate for 20 minutes. Use the pastry to line a deep 20cm metal flan tin and chill for a further 10 minutes.

Preheat the oven to 190°C (375°F). Line the pastry with baking paper and baking beans, then bake blind for 10–12 minutes. Carefully remove the paper and beans and bake the pastry for a further 5 minutes. Set aside, then reduce the oven temperature to 180°C (350°F).

In a jug, beat together the milk, egg yolks and garlic and season to taste. Spread the mustard over the base of the pastry and sprinkle over the Cheddar. Arrange the tomatoes and Brie on top and pour over the egg mixture. Cook for 30–35 minutes, until just set and golden. For the herb oil, mix all the ingredients together and drizzle over the tart. Serve warm.

Mushroom and Black Olive Risotto

serves 4

25g (¾oz) dried porcini
  mushrooms

3 tablespoons olive oil

1 onion, chopped

225g (8oz) large open
  mushrooms, chopped

1½ cup Arborio rice

450mL (15fl oz) vegetable stock

2 tablespoons black olives, pitted
  and roughly chopped

salt and black pepper

2 tablespoons black olive paste

fresh Parmesan to serve

Cover the porcini with 200mL (7fl oz) boiling water, then leave to soak for 20 minutes. Drain, reserving the water, and set aside. Heat the oil in a large heavy-based saucepan, add the onion and fresh mushrooms and fry for 4–5 minutes. Add the rice and stir to coat with the oil. Fry for 1–2 minutes.

Add the porcini and the reserved liquid to the rice with 225mL of the vegetable stock and the olives. Simmer, covered but stirring occasionally, for 10 minutes or until the liquid has been absorbed.

Stir in 100mL (3½fl oz) of the stock and cook for 5 minutes, covered, until absorbed. Add the rest of the stock, the seasoning and the olive paste and cook for 5 minutes, uncovered, stirring constantly. Remove from the heat and leave to rest, covered, for 5 minutes. Shave over the Parmesan, using a vegetable peeler, then serve.

Mushroom Pizza

serves 4

400g (14oz) canned chopped tomatoes

2 tablespoons olive oil

250g (9oz) mushrooms, wiped and thinly sliced

2 small cloves garlic, finely chopped

salt and black pepper

1 teaspoon dried oregano

2 x 23cm (9in) pizza bases

2 tablespoons finely grated Parmesan

150g (5oz) mozzarella, roughly chopped

Put the tomatoes into a saucepan and cook over a medium heat for 15–20 minutes, stirring from time to time, until the sauce has reduced and thickened.

Put the oil into a frying pan and heat over a medium heat for 1 minute. Add the mushrooms, garlic, salt, pepper and oregano and cook, stirring from time to time, for 7–10 minutes, until tender.

Meanwhile, preheat the oven to the highest setting—usually 240°C (465°F). Lay the pizza bases side by side on a large baking tray. Pour half of the tomato sauce onto each base and spread to the edges, using the back of a spoon.

Scatter half of the cooked mushroom mixture evenly over each pizza. Sprinkle over the Parmesan and scatter the mozzarella on top. Bake for 8–10 minutes, until the mozzarella is golden and the topping is bubbling.

Penne with Peppers and Mascarpone

serves 4

2 tablespoons olive oil

1 clove garlic, crushed

2 red onions, chopped

1 red, 1 yellow and 1 green
   capsicum (bell pepper),
   deseeded and cut into 1cm
   (⅓in) pieces

275g (9½oz) dried penne

200g (7oz) mascarpone

juice of ½ lemon

4 tablespoons fresh flat-leaf
   parsley, chopped

black pepper

4 tablespoons freshly grated
   Parmesan

Heat the oil in a large frying pan and fry the garlic, onions and capsicum for 10 minutes, stirring frequently, or until the vegetables have softened. Bring a large saucepan of salted water to the boil, add the pasta and cook for 8 minutes or until just firm in the centre (al dente). Drain, set aside and keep warm.

Stir half the mascarpone, the lemon juice, parsley and seasoning into the capsicum mixture. Cook for 5 minutes or until the mascarpone melts.

Stir the remaining mascarpone into the pasta, then add to the capsicum mixture, tossing together well. Serve with a sprinkling of Parmesan.

Tortellini with Tomato Cream Sauce

serves 4

50g (1¾oz) unsalted butter

1 small onion, very finely chopped

1 stick celery, very finely chopped

400mL (14fl oz) tomato purée

½ teaspoon caster (superfine) sugar

150mL (5fl oz) crème fraîche

salt and black pepper

600g (21oz) fresh spinach and ricotta tortellini

freshly grated Parmesan to serve

Place the butter, onion, celery, tomato purée and sugar in a heavy-based saucepan and bring to the boil. Reduce the heat and simmer, uncovered, for 30 minutes or until the vegetables have softened and the sauce thickened.

Spoon in the crème fraîche, season and bring back to the boil, stirring. Simmer for 1 minute, then add more salt and pepper if necessary.

Bring a large saucepan of salted water to the boil, add the pasta and cook for 2–3 minutes or until just firm in the centre (al dente), then drain. Transfer to a warmed serving bowl and pour over the sauce. Serve with Parmesan.

Roasted Vegetable Couscous

serves 4

4 parsnips, cut into chunks

salt

2 sweet potatoes, cut into chunks

4 turnips, quartered

2 cloves garlic, crushed

5 tablespoons olive oil

4 tablespoons apple or redcurrant jelly

300g (10½oz) couscous

500g (1lb) tomatoes, chopped

handful each of fresh parsley, chives and basil, chopped

juice of 1 lemon

300g (10½oz) broccoli, cut into florets

Preheat the oven to 200°C (400°F). Cook the parsnips in a saucepan of boiling salted water for 2 minutes, then drain. Place in a roasting tin with the sweet potatoes, turnips, garlic and 3 tablespoons of oil, turning to coat. Sprinkle with salt, then cook for 30 minutes or until lightly browned.

Melt the apple or redcurrant jelly in a pan with 4 tablespoons of water for 2–3 minutes, until it turns syrupy. Turn the vegetables in the tin and carefully cover with the syrup. Return to the oven for 10 minutes or until browned and glossy.

Meanwhile, prepare the couscous according to the packet instructions. Heat the rest of the oil in a frying pan and cook the tomatoes for 2–3 minutes, until softened. Add the couscous and heat through, then mix in the herbs and lemon juice. Meanwhile, boil the broccoli florets for 2 minutes or until tender, then drain. Serve the couscous with the roasted vegetables and broccoli arranged on top.

Risotto with Spinach and Gorgonzola

serves 6

4 cups vegetable stock

2 tablespoons olive oil

2 cloves garlic, crushed

1 onion, finely chopped

2 cups Arborio rice

½ cup white wine

220g (7¾oz) baby spinach

220g (7¾oz) Gorgonzola cheese,
   in small pieces

salt and freshly ground pepper

Place stock in a saucepan and bring to the boil. Leave simmering.

Heat oil in a large saucepan, add garlic and onion, and cook for 5 minutes, or until soft. Add rice, and stir, until well coated.

Pour in wine, and cook, until the liquid has been absorbed. Add a ladle of the stock, stir continuously, until the liquid has been absorbed, then add the next ladle of stock. Keep adding stock this way, and stirring, until all the stock is used, and until the rice is cooked, but still a little firm to bite.

Add the spinach, cheese and seasonings, stir, and cook, until spinach is just wilted and cheese has melted. Serve immediately.

Glamorgan Sausages with Tomato Salad

serves 4

100g (3½oz) potato

salt and black pepper

100g (3½oz) white breadcrumbs

150g (5oz) Lancashire or
  Caerphilly cheese, grated

1 small leek, finely chopped

¼ teaspoon dried sage

1 tablespoon fresh parsley,
  chopped

pinch of cayenne pepper

1 medium egg, plus 2 egg yolks

3 tablespoons plain (all-purpose)
  flour

oil for shallow-frying

SALAD

3 tablespoons olive oil

2 teaspoons balsamic vinegar

pinch of brown sugar

150g (5oz) cherry tomatoes

1 red onion, thinly sliced

5cm (2in) piece cucumber, sliced

few fresh basil leaves

Cook the potato in boiling salted water for 15–20 minutes, until tender. Drain well, mash, then leave to cool for 15 minutes. Mix the cold mash with half the breadcrumbs, the cheese, leek, sage and parsley. Season with salt, pepper and cayenne. Bind together with the yolks. Using your hands, shape into 12 sausages. Cover and refrigerate for 1 hour.

Season the flour. Beat the whole egg. Dip the sausages into the seasoned flour, then into the beaten egg, then coat in the remaining breadcrumbs. Heat 5mm of oil in a large frying pan and fry half the sausages, turning, for 10 minutes or until golden brown. Drain on absorbent paper and keep warm while you cook the rest.

Meanwhile, make the salad. Whisk together the oil, vinegar and sugar. Halve the tomatoes and toss in the dressing with the onion, cucumber and basil. Season and serve with the sausages.

Noodles with Broccoli and Carrots

serves 6

250g (9oz) stir-fry noodles

3 tablespoons vegetable oil

2.5cm (1in) fresh root ginger, finely chopped

2 red chillies, deseeded and finely chopped

4 cloves garlic, finely sliced

2 onions, thinly sliced

2 tablespoons clear honey

300mL (10½fl oz) vegetable or white wine

3 tablespoons white wine vinegar

600g (21fl oz) broccoli, cut into florets

300g (10½oz) carrots, sliced into ribbons with a vegetable peeler

chopped fresh chives to garnish

Prepare the noodles according to the packet instructions, then drain. Heat the oil in a large wok or heavy-based frying pan, then add the ginger and chillies and stir-fry for 1–2 minutes to soften.

Add the garlic and onions and fry for 5–6 minutes, until the onions have browned. Stir in the honey and cook for 6–8 minutes, until the honey starts to caramelise.

Add the stock or wine and vinegar to the onion mixture. Bring to the boil, then reduce the heat and simmer, uncovered, for 8 minutes or until the liquid has slightly reduced. Stir in the broccoli and carrots, cover, and simmer for 8–10 minutes or until the vegetables are cooked but still crunchy.

Stir in the noodles and mix well. Cook, stirring, for 2–3 minutes until the noodles are hot and most of the liquid has evaporated. Sprinkle over the chives just before serving.

Potato Gnocchi

serves 4

1kg (2lb 3oz) old floury potatoes, scrubbed

1¾ cup plain flour

Place the potatoes in a pan with just enough water to cover them, cover and boil the potatoes until tender without letting them break up. Drain and peel. Mash and rub through a metal sieve.

As soon as the purée is cool enough to handle, beat in the flour, then as the dough stiffens, turn it out to knead on a floured board. Knead until you have a soft and elastic dough.

Flour your hands and work surface, take a handful of the dough and knead lightly. Roll dough into a sausage shape. Cut into 2cm (¾in) slices.

Take a large, slim-pronged fork with round edges, wooden is best. Hold it in your left hand with the prongs down. Take a slice of dough and gently press it against the prongs with your thumb, letting the gnocchi roll off on to a clean cloth. Repeat with remaining dough. The gnocchi should curl up into crescent-shaped, ribbed shells as they roll off the fork. Alternatively, press each slice of dough gently around your finger to curve it, using a fork to make the ribbed grooves. The shaping thins out the centre of the gnocchi so that they cook evenly, and the grooves trap the flavours of the sauce.

Drop the gnocchi (about 20 at a time) into a large pan of boiling salted water. They will float to the surface when ready. Cook them just another 10 seconds, remove with a slotted spoon to a warm dish and sprinkle with freshly grated parmesan and butter and toss lightly. Serve immediately.

Pasta with Goat's Cheese

serves 4

1 tablespoon sunflower oil

25g (¾oz) butter

2 red onions, thinly sliced

1 clove garlic, finely chopped

sea salt

275g (9½oz) dried pasta, such as penne

250g (9oz) bunch asparagus, trimmed and cut into small pieces

150g (5oz) peas, fresh or frozen

200g (7oz) goat's cheese, roughly crumbled

freshly ground black pepper

Heat the oil and butter in a frying pan, and cook the onion over a medium heat for 7 minutes, stirring occasionally. Add the garlic and cook for a further 3 minutes, until the onions are golden and crisp.

Meanwhile, bring a large saucepan of salted water to the boil. Add the pasta and cook for 5 minutes, add the asparagus and cook for a further 2 minutes, add the peas and cook for 2 minutes. When cooked, drain well.

Return the pasta and vegetables to the saucepan and gently stir through nearly all of the onions, saving a small amount for garnish. Add the goat's cheese and plenty of freshly ground black pepper and mix together well. Serve topped with the remaining crispy onions.

Linguine with Leeks and Mushrooms

serves 4

500g (1lb) leeks, sliced

275g (9½oz) button mushrooms, sliced

1 bay leaf

40g (1½oz) butter

40g (1½oz) plain flour

2 cups milk

2 tablespoons snipped fresh chives, plus extra to garnish

black pepper

500g (1lb) fresh linguine

Steam the leeks and mushrooms with the bay leaf over a saucepan of boiling water for 10–15 minutes, until tender. Discard the bay leaf and keep the vegetables warm.

Melt the butter in a pan, add the flour and cook gently for 1 minute, stirring. Remove from the heat and gradually add the milk. Return to the heat and bring to the boil, stirring, until thickened. Reduce the heat and simmer for 2 minutes, stirring. Add the vegetables, chives and black pepper and heat through.

Bring a large saucepan of salted water to the boil, add the pasta and cook for 8 minutes or until just firm in the centre (al dente). Drain and return to the pan, then add the leek and mushroom sauce and toss lightly to mix. Garnish with fresh chives.

Bean and Vegetable Moussaka

serves 4

75g (2½oz) continental lentils, rinsed and drained

1 eggplant (aubergine), thinly sliced

2 tablespoons olive oil

2 leeks, sliced

2 sticks celery, chopped

2 cloves garlic, crushed

1 yellow capsicum (bell pepper), deseeded and diced

400g (14oz) canned chopped tomatoes

5 tablespoons dry white wine

2 tablespoons tomato purée

400g (14oz) canned black-eye beans, drained and rinsed

2 teaspoons dried mixed herbs

black pepper

300g (10½oz) natural yoghurt

2 medium eggs

25g (¾oz) Parmesan, finely grated

fresh herbs, such as basil, to garnish

Add the lentils to a saucepan of boiling water, cover and simmer for 30 minutes or until tender. Drain, rinse, then drain again and set aside.

Meanwhile, cook the eggplant slices in a saucepan of boiling water for 2 minutes. Drain, pat dry with absorbent paper and set aside.

Heat the oil in a frying pan, add the leeks, celery, garlic and capsicum and cook for 5 minutes or until slightly softened. Add the cooked lentils, tomatoes, wine, tomato purée, beans, mixed herbs and black pepper. Cover and bring to the boil, then simmer for 10 minutes or until the vegetables have softened.

Preheat the oven to 180°C (350°F). Spoon half the bean and lentil mixture into a shallow ovenproof dish and layer over half the eggplant. Repeat. Mix together the yoghurt and eggs and pour over the top. Sprinkle over the Parmesan. Cook for 40 minutes or until golden brown and bubbling. Garnish with fresh herbs.

Green Vegetable Stir-Fry

serves 4

2 tablespoons sesame seeds

2 tablespoons peanut oil

1 clove garlic, roughly chopped

2.5cm (1in) piece fresh root
   ginger, finely chopped

150g (5oz) broccoli, cut into very
   small florets

2 zucchini (courgette), halved
   lengthwise and finely sliced

170g (6oz) snowpeas

1 tablespoon rice wine or
   medium-dry sherry

1 tablespoon dark soy sauce

Heat a wok. Add the sesame seeds and dry-fry for 2 minutes or until golden, shaking the pan frequently. Remove and set aside.

Add the oil to the wok, heat for 1 minute, then add the garlic and ginger and stir-fry over a medium heat for 1–2 minutes, until softened. Add the broccoli and stir-fry for a further 2–3 minutes.

Add the zucchini and snowpeas and stir-fry for 3 minutes. Pour over the rice wine or sherry and sizzle for a minute. Add the soy then stir-fry for 2 minutes. Sprinkle over the toasted sesame seeds just before serving.

Chilli Mushroom Stir-Fry Noodles

serves 4

15g (½oz) dried porcini mushrooms

200g (7oz) fresh Chinese noodles

2 tablespoons sunflower oil

4 cloves garlic, sliced

1 red chilli, deseeded and chopped

2 teaspoons finely grated fresh ginger

450g (15oz) mixed fresh mushrooms, quartered or sliced

4 spring onions, sliced

4 tablespoons sake or dry sherry

4 tablespoons dark soy sauce

2 tablespoons lemon juice

1 tablespoon sugar

2 tablespoons fresh coriander (cilantro), chopped

Cover the dried mushrooms with 75mL (2½fl oz) of boiling water and soak for 15 minutes or until softened. Strain and reserve the liquid, then slice the mushrooms. Meanwhile, cook the noodles according to the packet instructions, until tender but still firm to the the bite, then drain.

Heat the oil in a wok or large frying pan until smoking, then add the garlic, chilli and ginger and stir-fry for 15 seconds or until they release their flavours. Add all the mushrooms and stir-fry for 2 minutes or until softened.

Add the spring onions, sake or sherry, soy sauce, lemon juice, sugar, coriander, reserved soaking liquid from the porcini mushrooms and the noodles, and heat for 1–2 minutes, until warmed through.

Vegetable Pizza

serves 4

1 tablespoon olive oil

2 small red onions, sliced

1 yellow capsicum (bell pepper), deseeded and sliced

2 small zucchini (courgette), sliced

1 clove garlic, crushed

225g (8oz) wholemeal flour

2 teaspoons baking powder

50g (1¾oz) butter

100mL (3½fl oz) milk

5 tablespoons tomato purée

2 teaspoons dried mixed herbs

black pepper

3 small Roma tomatoes, sliced

100g (3½oz) aged Cheddar, grated

fresh basil to garnish (optional)

Preheat the oven to 220°C (420°F). Heat the oil in a saucepan, then add the onions, capsicum, zucchini and garlic and cook for 5 minutes or until softened, stirring occasionally. Set aside.

Place the flour and baking powder in a bowl, then rub in the butter. Stir in the milk to form a smooth dough and knead lightly.

Roll out the dough on a lightly floured surface to a circle about 25cm (10in) wide and place on a buttered baking sheet. Mix together the tomato purée, mixed herbs and black pepper and spread over the dough. Top with the onion mixture.

Arrange the tomato slices on top and sprinkle with Cheddar. Bake for 25–30 minutes, until the cheese is golden brown and bubbling. Garnish with fresh basil if using.

Pumpkin, Lemon and Parmesan Risotto

serves 4

4 cups vegetable stock

large pinch of saffron threads

2 tablespoons olive oil

15g (½oz) butter

1 onion, chopped

1 clove garlic, finely chopped

2 cups Arborio rice

1kg (2lb 3oz) pumpkin or
 butternut squash, deseeded and
 cut into 2cm (¾in) pieces

150mL (5fl oz) dry white wine

salt and black pepper

grated zest and juice of 1 lemon

50g (1¾oz) Parmesan, grated

½ teaspoon fresh rosemary, finely
 chopped

Heat 300mL (10½fl oz) of the stock in a saucepan until boiling, then remove the pan from the heat and stir in the saffron threads.

Heat the oil and butter in a large heavy-based pan and gently fry the onion and garlic for 4–5 minutes, until softened but not browned. Add the rice and pumpkin or squash to the pan, and stir for 2 minutes or until the rice is coated with oil.

Stir in the wine and boil for a few seconds to cook off the alcohol, then pour in the saffron stock. Simmer, stirring constantly, for 5 minutes or until the stock has been absorbed. Add half the remaining stock and cook, stirring, for 10 minutes or until absorbed. Add the remaining stock and cook, stirring, for a further 10 minutes or until the rice is tender but still firm to the bite. Season.

Stir the lemon zest and juice and the Parmesan into the risotto, then garnish with rosemary.

Zucchini (Courgette) and Cheese Gratin

serves 4

4 large zucchini (courgette), sliced diagonally

400g (14oz) canned chopped tomatoes

2 tablespoons fresh basil, shredded

sea salt and freshly ground black pepper

250g (9oz) Italian mozzarella, drained and sliced

15g (½oz) freshly grated Parmesan

1 tablespoon extra virgin olive oil

Preheat the oven to 200°C (400°F). Blanch the zucchini in boiling water for about 4 minutes, drain well and then thoroughly dry them using absorbent paper.

Drain the canned tomatoes in a sieve to remove all excess liquid. Layer half the zucchini in a shallow, ovenproof dish, spread with half the sieved tomatoes, then sprinkle with half the basil and a little seasoning. Place half of the mozzarella slices on top in an even layer.

Repeat the layers once again, sprinkle with Parmesan, drizzle with olive oil and then cook for about 25 minutes.

Cappellini with Tomatoes and Basil

serves 4-6

½ cup olive oil

6 cloves garlic, thinly sliced

550g (1lb 3oz) Roma tomatoes, deseeded and diced

⅓ cup basil, shredded

salt

freshly ground black pepper

400g (14oz) cappellini

Heat half the oil in a pan, add the garlic, and cook over a medium heat, until the garlic is slightly browned and golden.

Reduce the heat, and add tomatoes, basil, salt and pepper, and cook for 5 minutes (or until tomatoes are just heated through). Bring a large saucepan of salted water to the boil, add the pasta and cook for 8 minutes or until just firm in the centre (al dente). Add remaining oil to the cooked pasta.

Serve tomato mixture over cappellini pasta.

Sabzee

serves 4

large handful of English spinach
leaves

½ bunch coriander (cilantro)

8 large parsley sprigs

10 large dill sprigs

2 green spring onions

2 tablespoons extra virgin olive
oil

pinch of salt

2 pita breads

½ cup plain yoghurt, seasoned
with a pinch of cayenne

Wash the spinach leaves thoroughly and trim
away the stalks below the leaves. Wash the herbs
thoroughly and remove larger stems. Chop all
roughly and toss with onions and just enough oil
to barely coat. Cut the pita breads in half and line
each half with the yoghurt before stuffing them
with the greens. Additional yoghurt can be served
on the side for dipping the sandwich into.

Asparagus, Ricotta And Herb Frittata

serves 4

450g (15oz) fresh asparagus

12 medium eggs

2 small cloves garlic, crushed

4 tablespoons fresh mixed herbs, including basil, chives and parsley, chopped

salt and black pepper

50g (1¾oz) butter

100g (3½oz) ricotta

squeeze of lemon juice

olive oil or truffle oil to drizzle

Parmesan to serve

fresh chives to garnish

Preheat the grill to high. Place the asparagus in a grill pan and grill for 10 minutes or until charred and tender, turning once. Keep warm.

Meanwhile, whisk together the eggs, garlic, herbs and seasoning. Melt 25g (¾oz) of the butter in an ovenproof frying pan until it starts to foam, then immediately pour in a quarter of the egg mixture and cook for 1–2 minutes, stirring occasionally, until almost set.

Place under the preheated grill for 3–4 minutes, until the egg is cooked through and the top of the frittata is set, then transfer to a plate. Keep warm while you make the 3 remaining frittatas, adding more butter when necessary.

Arrange a quarter of the asparagus and a quarter of the ricotta over each frittata, squeeze over the lemon juice, season and drizzle with oil. Top with shavings of Parmesan and garnish with fresh chives.

Vegetable Chilli Bake

serves 4

1 tablespoon sunflower oil

1 onion, chopped

1 green capsicum (bell pepper), deseeded and diced

2 cloves garlic, finely chopped

1 large green chilli, deseeded and finely chopped

2 teaspoons ground cumin

1 teaspoon hot chilli powder

400g (14oz) canned chopped tomatoes

1 tablespoon tomato purée

3 carrots, cubed

175g (6oz) swede, cubed

175g (6oz) mushrooms, chopped

3 sticks celery, finely chopped

6 tablespoons vegetable stock

black pepper

420g (14¾oz) canned red kidney beans, drained and rinsed

fresh coriander (cilantro) to garnish

Preheat the oven to 180°C (350°F). Heat the oil in a large flameproof and ovenproof casserole dish. Add the onion, green capsicum, garlic and green chilli and cook for 5 minutes or until softened, stirring occasionally.

Add the cummsin and chilli powder and cook, stirring gently for 1 minute to release the flavours. Mix in the tomatoes, tomato purée, carrots, swede, mushrooms, celery, stock and black pepper.

Cover and cook in the oven for 45 minutes, stirring once. Add the kidney beans, cover again and cook for a further 15–20 minutes or until all the vegetables are tender. Garnish with fresh coriander.

Root Vegetable Curry

1 tablespoon olive oil

1 onion, chopped

1 green chilli, deseeded and finely
   chopped

1 clove garlic, finely chopped

2.5cm (1in) piece fresh root
   ginger, finely chopped

2 tablespoons plain (all-purpose)
   flour

2 teaspoons each ground
   coriander, ground cumin and
   turmeric

300mL (10½fl oz) vegetable stock

200mL (7fl oz) tomato purée

750g (1lb 10oz) mixed root
   vegetables, such as potato,
   sweet potato, celeriac and
   swede, cubed

2 carrots, thinly sliced

black pepper

chopped fresh coriander (cilantro)
   garnish

Heat the oil in a large saucepan. Add the onion, chilli, garlic and ginger and cook for 5 minutes or until softened, stirring occasionally. Stir in the flour, ground coriander, cumin and turmeric and cook gently, stirring, for 1 minute to release the flavours.

Gradually stir in the stock, then add the tomato purée, cubed root vegetables and the carrots, season with black pepper and mix well.

Bring to the boil, stirring, then cover, reduce the heat and simmer for 45 minutes or until the vegetables are tender, stirring occasionally. Garnish with fresh coriander.

Index

UK £ 9.99
USA $14.99